Praise for *When]*

When Prayer Becomes a Lifest
and her personal encounters ...
prayer life. As I read through it, it sparked a desire for me to seek out the lover of my soul—the Holy Spirit and rekindle our fellowship, and I trust that will be your experience as well.
– **Olusegun Akinkugbe**, City of God, Glasgow

This book will change your thinking about communicating with the Father. Pastor Imisi eloquently breaks down how one can imbibe a life of prayer in a compelling and relatable manner.
– **Joycee Awosika**, CEO, ORÍKÌ Group.

When Prayer Becomes a Lifestyle debunks the myths about prayer and establishes the truth about living a prayerful life in a simple and progressive manner. In this book, the author takes us on an enthralling journey through the scriptures and her personal prayer life as she shares pragmatic tips to help the reader rekindle a fire for intimacy with the Father. As you read chapter after chapter, you will develop a desire for a deeper communion with God, and in fact put on the graceful garment of prayer because it looks good on you!

I count it a privilege to have been one of the first readers of this life-changing book. It opened my eyes to see prayer beyond an act carried out at specific hours of the day. I became more aware of the access we have to the Father—one that is not hindered by my situation, timing, location or correctness of speech, but based on a relationship with a Father who loves and hears me. It is a must read!
– **Moji Ogunlola,** Lawyer/Copywriter

This is an intimate script on prayer. In this book, Imisi shares her journey and sound principles that can help us start or advance our prayer walk. Prayer is intimacy with God and this book shows us how to grow in oneness with the Father. It also provides the roadmap that would lead us straight to the heart of Jesus.

– **Samuel Mpamugo**, Business Strategist/Executive Coach

One thing I love about the book is its simplicity and the power each chapter carries. I am certain that people will be inspired to pray while reading like I was. *When Prayer Becomes a Lifestyle* opened my eyes to many things about prayer, and I got a few revelations especially the part where God conversed with Adam in his fallen state. It showed me that God wants to commune with us no matter what our state may be. He is such a loving Father. I also enjoyed how real and open she was, sharing her experiences and testimonies in the book. It is practical.

– **Mojisola Coker,** Media Practitioner/Worship Minister

A powerful book on prayer. Well-researched, Holy Spirit-inspired, and easy to read. I am sure anyone who reads it will begin to pray more effectively.

– **Tinuke Olashore**, CEO, PJK Nigeria Ltd.

When Prayer Becomes a Lifestyle

You are loved

WHEN PRAYER BECOMES A LIFESTYLE

prayer looks good on you

Imisioluwa Owolabi

PRIMA

ISBN: 978-978-56107-6-5

Published in Nigeria in 2019 by Narrative Landscape Press
under its Prima Imprint
9, Odunlami Street, Anthony Village, Lagos, Nigeria
07014522083, 09090554406 – 7
contact@narrativelandscape.com
www.narrativelandscape.com

A catalogue record for this book is available from the National Library of Nigeria.

Cover Design and Layout by Ayebabeledaipre Sokari
Cover Image and Author's Photo: TY Bello
Printed by Nutech Print Services

DEDICATION

To my dearest Father – Spiri Mi – a God that always shows up
A faithful Companion and Best friend
For all the times of laughter and happiness
For calling me and loving me before I even met Him
For all the Spirit inspired thoughts and ideas
Including this book
I'm eternally grateful.

I also dedicate this book to my biological sister, Fikayo Adeyinka. I am a product of your commitment to God. While I read a lot about living a Christian life, you showed me what it meant to be a Christian and made it easy to follow your footsteps. You inspired me to say YES to Jesus and be sold out to Him. You were the first Bible I read. I am who I am today because of your sacrifices and love for God. You will always be my hero. Love you sis.

FOREWORD

I met Imisi about five years ago and I could instantly see there was "something" about her. The French would say "Je ne sais quoi", *I do not know what.* But it is that distinct quality that sets something apart. You could just see God had His hand on her life. Her childlike enthusiasm, her boundless joy and her inquisitive mind ever ready to learn were all infectious—you only have to meet her once to know what I am talking about. Ever since then, we have had a wonderful relationship. Let me introduce you to g-daughter (god daughter). I am affectionately referred to as g-papa (god father). We laugh and rib each other from our respective locations: she in Nigeria, and I in England.

More than the boundless joy she exudes, Imisi loves God; she loves Jesus and is not afraid to tell it from the rooftop or mountains. There is so much more I could say about this extraordinary woman. As you read this book, *When Prayer Becomes a Lifestyle*, I guarantee you will also see Imisi's essence as a person. You will understand her relationship with God and why He is using her to inspire her generation.

In *When Prayer Becomes a Lifestyle,* Imisi takes us on an inspirational journey on prayer. The pages are full of insightful wisdom, engaging anecdotes and practical steps to invigorate your prayer life. The book is so engaging it belies her age. Indeed, she is an old soul! No wonder she is on the cutting edge of what God is doing today. G-daughter you knocked this one out of the park! This is a must-read for whoever is despondent about their "walk" and "talk" with God. Happy reading.

Dr Edward A. Addison
Pastor/Leadership Consultant

INTRODUCTION

Staring at the sky one evening about twenty years ago, I whispered to God, "If you are there, let me fall from the stool." (I honestly do not know why this was the evidence I asked for). I fell from the stool, either because I wanted to or under the unction of the Holy Ghost. I kept staring at the sky, conversing with someone I believed was God. It was so beautiful that night, and from that day, I would often look up to the sky, knowing that He was right there. This became a habit, and God and I had our spot – the sky. Sometimes, I would just mumble words aloud so He could hear me. I believe this was the beginning of my prayer relationship with God that began as a conversation between us. I felt He lured me to Him. I believe that we would notice Him calling, if only we paid attention to our environment.

The reality is that prayer is a conversation between God and me regardless of the situation. It does not matter whether I am engaging in warfare against the devil, seeking His counsel or even praying about boys. Thinking about prayer this way, made it easy for me. I mean, how hard can it be conversing with a friend that I love? I came to understand these truths about prayer a few years after I consciously began my journey with God, and it revolutionised my beliefs about prayer.

Prayer can really look good on us.

CONTENTS

DEDICATION ***vi***

FOREWORD ***ix***

INTRODUCTION ***xi***

CHAPTER I

In the Beginning: Myths and Truths About Prayer ***1***

CHAPTER II

A Child-Like Heart ***13***

CHAPTER III

The Untold Story of David, The Man After God's Heart ***25***

CHAPTER IV

Jesus, Our Intercessor and Ultimate Prayer Model ***37***

CHAPTER V

We Have Work to Do ***61***

CHAPTER VI
Prayer Looks Good on You ***87***

ADDITIONAL CHAPTER RESOURCES ***95***

RECOMMENDED BOOKS/REFERENCES ***103***

ACKNOWLEDGEMENT ***105***

ABOUT THE AUTHOR ***107***

I

In the Beginning: Myths and Truths About Prayer

"

... we cannot **pray effectively** without the help of God.

"

Prayer is not a tool for controlling God; rather, it is an invitation to fellowship with God, which engenders intimacy and a strong foundation for an effective prayer life.

Often, people say to me, "Imisi, please pray for me." I consider this a big honour and I respond, "I will pray with you." However, when someone says something like, "Imisi pray for me because I know God will hear you more" or "I'm not sure if He will hear me", my response changes because God is no respecter of persons. If He hears me, He will hear you too. This is the first misconception that I want to debunk, that God only answers some people, or one needs an intermediary to reach Him. Under the dispensation of grace, the above viewpoints are wrong. When it comes to praying, the question is: do you believe? This is because Jesus Christ has redeemed us from the curse of the law and we now have direct access to the Father.

God created the offices of the fivefold ministry (pastor, teacher, evangelist, prophet and apostle), and the responsibilities of these ministers are to edify us and direct us to God. It is not to return us to the days where only the priests could enter the Holy of Holies or the prophets could hear God for us.

> 11 And [His gifts to the church were varied and] He Himself appointed some as apostles [special messengers, representatives], some as prophets [who speak a new message from God to the people], some as evangelists [who spread the good news of salvation], and some as pastors and teachers [to shepherd and guide and instruct],
>
> 12 [and He did this] to fully equip and perfect the saints (God's people) for works of service, to build up the body of Christ [the church];
>
> 13 until we all reach oneness in the faith and in the knowledge of the Son of God, [growing spiritually] to become a mature believer, reaching to the measure of the fullness of Christ [manifesting His spiritual completeness and exercising our spiritual gifts in unity] (Ephesians 4:11–13 Amplified version).

Do not get me wrong, there is a place for their guidance, discipleship, intercession and ministrations, but they are meant to bring us closer to God, not drive us away from Him and into dependence on man. Like the scripture above says, these offices are meant to build us till we become like Jesus Christ. I love what Hebrews 4:16 says, "Let us therefore come boldly to the throne of grace, that we may obtain mercy and find grace to help in time of need." Thank God for salvation. We have been reconciled with the Father, to the way it was and the way He intended it to be from the very beginning.

Let us walk back to the beginning where conversations between God and man was first recorded in the Bible. This took place in Genesis 3:8–13.

> 8 And they heard the sound of the Lord God walking in the garden in the cool of the day, and Adam and his wife hid themselves from the presence of the Lord God among the trees of the garden.
>
> 9 Then the Lord God called to Adam and said to him, "Where are you?"

10 So he said, "I heard Your voice in the garden, and I was afraid because I was naked; and I hid myself."

11 And He said, "Who told you that you were naked? Have you eaten from the tree of which I commanded you that you should not eat?"

12 Then the man said, "The woman whom You gave to be with me, she gave me of the tree, and I ate."

13 And the Lord God said to the woman, "What is this you have done?" The woman said, "The serpent deceived me, and I ate."

Verse eight says they heard the sound of the Lord God walking in the garden in the cool of the day. To recognise the sound of God walking in the garden, Adam and Eve must have been familiar with the sound, meaning that communicating with Him must have been their custom. In verse nine, we see the start of a conversation between God calling out to Adam, and in verse ten, Adam responding to God, indicating a close relationship building between them. Therefore, we can see that prayer originated from God, starting with Adam and Eve; hence, we cannot pray effectively without the help of God. Invariably, fellowship with God breeds intimacy, and intimacy fuels trust in prayer.

The backdrop of prayer from Genesis three is not a picture of an angry God yelling at them despite what they had done; rather, He is conversing with them, giving them a chance to speak to Him. He made provision for the saviour and condemned the devil.

What I love most about this story is the setting. The first time we see a long dialogue between God and man is in man's fallen state. The devil had tempted the woman to eat from the Tree of the Knowledge of Good and Evil, which God had instructed them not to eat. Though God knew what had happened in the garden, He went ahead to fellowship with them. He is a Father indeed, because he gives even in the judgment. He made provision for the saviour and condemned the devil. The point is that you are never too far gone to respond to God's love. You are never too condemned to pray or talk to God. Even in your fallen state, if you ask for His mercy or cry out to Him, He will hear you because He has already paid the price for your redemption. The question is: what will you do with this offer? Will you embrace His redemptive plan or toss it aside and continue in sin?

You can call on your Father because He died for you so that you can have unhindered access to Him without any human intermediary. Would you not love to enjoy that level of intimacy with God "in the cool of the day"? No matter how much you mature in prayer, you cannot pray effectively without the help of the Holy Spirit. So, quit trying to pray without His help or else you will keep struggling. We must make the effort and schedule the time to pray, but not independent of God. Remember, He invented prayer.

Let us start by understanding some fundamental truths concerning prayer as laid out in the Bible:

- Prayer was originated by God who is an amazing Father (Genesis 3:8-13).
- God wants to answer our prayers (Jeremiah 29:12; 33:3; Psalms 145:18, Isaiah 65:24). (Get one scripture that speaks to you the most about God answering prayers and meditate on it).
- Prayer must be backed up by faith (Mark 11:24; James 1:6-7). (It is not enough to ask in faith, but we must also keep from wavering in our faith or from doubting).
- Intimacy changes how we see prayer and how we pray (John 15; 15:7).

- Knowing our identity helps us to pray effectively (Romans 8:14-17).
- Our prayer should come from a place of victory (Romans 8:37; I John 5:4).

A. How to Pray: An Approach

The scriptures below demonstrate how we are to offer prayers and approach the throne room in this dispensation.

- We come in the name of the Lord and we direct our prayers to God (John 16:23-24; John 14:6; John 15:16).
- We come boldly and confidently (Ephesians 3:12; Hebrews 4:16).
- We understand that it is a dialogue. God is more eager to speak to us than we can imagine; however, we must always be led by the Spirit because sometimes we are to simply be quiet and soak ourselves in His presence. It is the same way that sometimes when we approach our earthly fathers, we just listen to them (Isaiah 1:18; Rev 3:20; John 10:27).

  Don't be afraid to ask. John Wesley said, "It seems God is limited by our prayer life—that He can do nothing for humanity unless someone asks Him" (Matthew 7:7).

B. To Whom Do We Pray?

God is the only one to whom we pray. After this manner therefore pray ye: Our Father which art in heaven, hallowed be thy name (Mathew 6:9). However, there is one truth that is fundamental to effectively engaging the mysteries of prayer. It affects how you see and relate with God as well as how you interpret your outcomes. We shall explore it in the next chapter.

REFLECTIONS

1. What does prayer mean to you?
2. Do you have any experience(s) that have either hindered or heightened your belief in prayer?
3. What does the Bible say about any of the experiences you have had?

II

A Child-Like Heart

"

The **childlike heart** is one that **is never ashamed** to go back to God . . .

"

To properly illustrate this chapter, I will start by sharing some stories.

I must have been about thirteen years old or less when a serious incident happened. I remember the night vividly, and whenever it crosses my mind, it still makes me laugh. Our neighbours teased me for months afterwards. I was heading to the restroom, half frustrated because of the power outage. Trying to stay alert, I walked past the candle in the passage when I noticed that the toilet door was ajar. I wondered who left it open. Then, I realised that I was home alone with my dad whom I had not seen in a while. I discovered him almost lifeless on the floor, and while I was trying to lift him to a sitting position, he passed out. In shock and unsure of what to do, I shook him continuously and prayed, "God please bring him back to life." Then I left him and ran to our neighbour's house – inappropriately dressed, hence the teasing – screaming at the top of my voice, "Help, help, my dad is dying!" I got the attention of a doctor and many other neighbours, and fortunately, my dad was rushed to the hospital in time for his life to be saved.

Another time when my dad fainted, I ran towards him, holding and rocking him because it felt like he was lifeless as he took a deep breath and stopped breathing. With tears in my eyes I cried and prayed, "Lord, save my father," and miraculously he started breathing and we rushed him to the hospital. These experiences did something to my core. I knew nothing about waiting on someone to pray for me nor did I wonder if I was qualified to call on God. I believed we were friends since we conversed from time to time, besides, I did not have the luxury of time to wait for someone to pray on my behalf. I lifted my voice and believed that He would answer me. This was another layer of foundation that was added to my beliefs about prayer.

I remember when my parents no longer had a car and I was too tired to walk to school. I would quietly ask God to align my path with my friends whose parents had cars on the way. Some days, I endured the scorching sun and walked the entire journey. I'd look up to the sky and say, "God na!" but that did not stop me from going back to Him to make the same request. On some other days, just when I thought there was no hope, I would hear a horn behind me. I would smile and enter the car, but in my heart, I would blow Him kisses. These experiences made me believe that He sees my heart and knows my little requests. Nothing goes unnoticed before Him and so I learnt to thank Him for little things. It strengthened our bond even more.

Has this ever happened to you? Where your family had only one electrical output or phase, so if power went out on that phase, you remained in darkness while your neighbours who had two or more outputs would switch phases and get power? This happened to me, and it was a devastating experience. I remember praying and asking God to restore our light; nothing was too big or small for me to talk to Him about. There were days when the power was restored without the NEPA officials fixing it. When that happened, I'd jump and celebrate and thank Him. There were days when the officials came over to fix it, and I was grateful that He made them come.

At a point as I got older, I started believing that I could "fix" everything by myself, and I stopped consulting God on my decisions. But things did not go so well with this new self-possessed independence. Rather than feel happy, I became miserable, so I repented and began to place it all at His feet again. We literally spent the day together; down to what I decided to wear that day. Don't get me wrong, God wants us to use our senses, but not independent of Him. He gave us the senses in the first place. Proverbs 3:5–6 says, in ALL of your ways, acknowledge Him.

Other lovely memories that come to mind are my birthday wishes. I have always been excited about my birthdays, even days when it rained cats and dogs with no cake or party food for consolation. I remember a particular year, I was really praying that I'd get to have a special birthday hairdo, and miraculously, someone in the hair salon paid for my special hairstyle without me asking. My brother also sent me two thousand naira. I remember one of my childhood friends, Nike Ayoigbala and me, sitting under the shade outside my house drinking Fanta and celebrating my birthday in the rain, but I was grateful. Even though I desired more, I was still grateful.

The point I am trying to make with these stories is that you should never lose your childlike heart in pursuit of God. Yes, we grow up, but do not trade that childlike heart that believes God against all odds—a heart that keeps believing in the face adversity, such that even when things do not work out as planned, you will thank God and trust again. It is important to maintain a heart that believes that the Father has a reason. A heart that can ask Him what went wrong, not to question His authority, but to learn and get better at handling things.

Contrary to what people believe, you can engage God. He is your Father and you can ask Him questions but do not question Him. There is a difference between asking God questions and questioning Him. Asking God questions is a desire to know more or get clarity over certain issues and direction (Matthew 17:19–21).

> 19 Then the disciples came to Jesus privately and said, "Why could we not cast it out?"
>
> 20 So Jesus said to them, "Because of your unbelief; for assuredly, I say to you, if you have faith as a mustard seed, you will say to this mountain, 'Move from here to there,' and it will move; and nothing will be impossible for you.

21 However, this kind does not go out except by prayer and fasting."

On the other hand, questioning God implies that you doubt his character or sovereignty (See Job 7:20; 38–39).

The childlike heart is one that is never ashamed to go back to God to ask for the same thing, cry for help or to repent. It is a heart that is always open to learning; one that constantly looks out to see the wonders of the Father.

Picture this: A little child who you just corrected or spanked will always come back to you or run into your arms like the incident never happened. Children are never too busy to play with you, and when they play hide and seek with you, they will not give up until they find you. We ought to be the same way with God, especially when it comes to prayer. It is about conversing, relating and fellowshipping with the Father. This is a fundamental truth we must know, believe and build upon or else we will act like orphans trying to please a master.

I still maintain a childish heart towards God. Though I mature in spiritual things, I will not trade a heart that never loses its sense of wonder. I am not ashamed to laugh, cry or stay silent in His presence.

I am not limited to just Sunday services to enjoy a good time with Him. I am His temple and I live forever for an audience of One.

Do not make your prayer life or relationship with God a public show, lacking depth or intimacy. If it is really what it is, the spotlight won't matter to you.

I love Amanda Cook's song, *Wonder*. The first verse says:

> May we never lose our wonder
> May we never lose our wonder
> Wide-eyed and mystified
> May we be just like a child
> Staring at the beauty of our King.

In case you are not yet convinced about the need for a childlike heart, let us see what the Scriptures say about it: "…assuredly, I say to you, unless you are converted and become as little children, you will by no means enter the kingdom of heaven" (Matthew 18:3).

So, what does it mean to be childlike? Having a childlike faith and heart is not the same as being childish; rather, a childlike heart is being conscious of the Father and looking around to see His wonder in all things. According to the Merriam Webster Dictionary, "childlike" can be marked by innocence, trust, and ingenuousness, for example, childlike delight.

A childlike heart with faith is one that is free of fear and the cares of this world; a heart that drops all the shenanigans that come with adulthood at the feet of God, becomes like a child, in total awe and trust of the Father. This attitude changes how you perceive and understand prayer. It ceases to just be an activity; rather, it becomes a lifestyle of intimacy and fellowship with God that is not constrained by time or a to-do list.

How to be like a child:

- Be trusting
- Do not bother about the cares of the world
- Be in awe of the Father
- Come in innocence and be forgiving
- Be humble and dependent on the Father
- Believe completely
- Be joyful
- Believe that the Father loves you
- Loves the Father with reckless abandon

You might say, "But I don't have all these stories or remember anything to make me feel like a child." I hear you dear friend, but guess what? There might be one memory of you and God. It could be the time you received Christ into your life or the day He saved you from a terrible incident, or the time you just had a good laugh. Ask the Holy Spirit to help you remember. If you truly don't have any, it is not too late to start creating memories with Him. Start by repenting. Drop all the baggage and ask God to help you experience what it means to have a childlike heart and faith. By the way, God and I still enjoy our sky conversations—I do not think I can ever outgrow that.

Please understand that this affects how you will view prayers, the results you will see and the possibility of inheriting the Kingdom of God. It is not a suggestion but a command.

Jesus said, "Let the little children come to Me, and do not forbid them; for of such is the kingdom of heaven" (Matthew 19:14).

REFLECTIONS

1. When last did you look out for the wonders of God in your life, your day or environment?
2. What is that childlike feeling you remember about your experience with God?
3. What do you intend to do from now to maintain your childlike heart before God?

III

The Untold Story of David, The Man After God's Heart

"

It is remarkable that **David still sought** after the face of **the Lord** despite the calamities that befell him.

"

I look forward to meeting David in heaven. He was a man of prayer, who had a childlike heart and was sincere about his flaws when dealing with God. He loved God. He was a giver and prayer looked good on him!

The Book of Psalms in the Bible expressed the emotions of David. These emotions varied from feelings of despair, discouragement and abandonment to hope, joy and excitement. David – the man who never lost a battle; the man after God's own heart – had these feelings most of us have today and he expressed them. But one thing was certain, David never remained in despair neither did he lose his heart of worship. Over time, as a result of his intimate relationship with God, he learnt how to encourage himself in the Lord in the face of fierce challenges (1 Samuel 30).

Picture this: you were rejected by your family, neglected by your allies and declared "Most Wanted" by the head of state whom you had helped and saved several times. You escaped a series of assassinations; you were rejected by former enemies who you had shown kindness, and when you got home, you found your whole estate on fire—many people had been robbed and kidnapped. As if that was not enough, the people who you had helped to establish, your trusted community, were plotting to kill you because the tragedy was unbearable. They forgot that your family members were also taken away as hostages. This was what happened to David.

What would you do if you were in David's shoes? I would not judge you if you said you would quit or behead those men to remind them who is boss. David did none of those things; instead, he requested for the ephod – a sleeveless garment worn by Jewish priests for prayers – and enquired of the Lord.

It is remarkable that David still sought after the face of the Lord despite the calamities that befell him. It was clear that he knew where his help laid, and he was too connected to his source to be overwhelmed by the problems at hand. Look at this short prayer (1 Samuel 30:8), "And David inquired of the Lord, saying, 'Shall I pursue this troop? Shall I overtake them?' The Lord answered him, 'Pursue, for you shall surely overtake them and without fail recover all.'" Oh Lord may nothing separate us from You, not even problems or difficult seasons.

The verse above confirms what was written in Romans 8:35, "Who shall separate us from the love of Christ? Shall tribulation, or distress, or persecution, or famine, or nakedness, or peril, or sword?" David lived this scripture even before it was written. Nothing should push you away from God. Your pain should drive you closer to God. We can deduce that David was willing to do whatever God instructed. The place of prayer is the place of clarity. Nothing should be too urgent that we cannot communicate or inquire of God, even if just for a second.

Another beautiful thing about the scripture is that God answered. He wants to answer your prayers. His answer might not be what you expect but it will always be what is best for you. It reminds me of how just like Jesus in Matthew 8:23–27, David was able to find peace in the storm. It was not a time for lengthy prayers, inspired by the Holy Ghost; rather, it was a time for dependency on the trust he had in God, which he had built over time.

The ability to be still and know He is God comes from a place of intimacy with him through prayers and fellowship.

Like David, how do we get to pray with trust, faith and hope in the face of adversity, so that the pain does not separate us from God but pushes us towards him? The years 2016 and 2017 were a trying time for my family. We made a huge investment in a legitimate business. It was such a good opportunity that we invited some of our close friends to partake in it so we could mutually raise the capital and enjoy the returns. We were already dreaming of the things we would do with the money and how we would reinvest a portion. What should have taken one week took almost two years. We lost our money and the funds of trusted friends and family. It was a devastating nightmare we had to go through.

Like David, we went through a rollercoaster of emotions. I went from feeling shocked, to calling the bluff of the devil because I was certain that in a few days, it would all be over. Two months later, we were paying off debts we had not bargained for. I was pained, upset and confused. I checked again, what went wrong? That was when the “buts” started rolling in: “but we prayed, but we heard ‘go ahead’, but, but, but…” However, through it all, we felt the comfort of God. At a point, we kept saying, "It could have been worse, but God came through for us." For almost two years, we had to keep diverting all personal funds to pay off debts, but the moment we moved our focus from the situation to God, we enjoyed His peace, and the unusual strength and joy that comes from an intimate relationship with Him.

When I remember the situation, I speak like a child, "I trust my father, He will compensate us, we will not just retrieve the money, we will get much more and bigger business opportunities." I tell my husband, "Please view this loss as an investment that we cannot touch the returns until a later time." This is the assurance I have in God. He is a restorer and He has done it before in times past. Like David, I can recount the moments He came through for us. Even though it may look inconsequential compared to the mountain ahead of me, I choose to remember; I choose to be encouraged, and this aids my prayer life. It moves me from praying from a place of bitterness to praying from a place of joy despite what has happened.

As I write, we are yet to retrieve the funds, but we have gotten more from God. His unending love, protection, shelter, the celebration of other victories, and the ability to make great sacrifices that have humbled us. We are confident that faithful is He that has begun the good work and we know He will perfect it. We know our testimony will be complete, because we have left the "how" to God. What we know is that we have been blessed beyond what looked lost and we will recover all in the way God deems best. We are hopeful.

I must add that my husband and I thank God for the experience. It has drawn us closer and further tightened our bond. We have grown deeper in God because we know the God of the storm never lets His beloved drown, and this has made our faith stronger. We laugh more and have learnt how to be more prudent with our resources. We can boldly declare that what the devil intended for evil, the Lord turned around for our good.

So, no matter what you are going through or will go through, you can still pray even if it is a whisper of love or a cry for help—put your trust and dependency in God. Let me add here that God did not call us to be macho or tough for him. Just like the father in Mark 9:20–27, it is okay to genuinely pray that God helps you overcome your unbelief. It demonstrates a level of vulnerability when you say, "Lord help me."

20 Then they brought him to Him. And when he saw Him, immediately the spirit convulsed him, and he fell on the ground and wallowed, foaming at the mouth.

21 So He asked his father, "How long has this been happening to him"? And he said, "From childhood.

22 And often he has thrown him both into the fire and into the water to destroy him. But if You can do anything, have compassion on us and help us."

23 Jesus said to him, "If you can believe, all things are possible to him who Believes."

24 Immediately the father of the child cried out and said with tears, "Lord, I believe; help my unbelief!"

25 When Jesus saw that the people came running together, He rebuked the unclean spirit, saying to it, "Deaf and dumb spirit, I command you, come out of him and enter him no more!"

26 Then the spirit cried out, convulsed him greatly, and came out of him. And he became as one dead, so that many said, "He is dead."

27 But Jesus took him by the hand and lifted him up, and he arose.

Afterwards, whatever He tells you to do, please do it. Take corresponding steps but if need be, do not ever feel ashamed to ask God for help. If we read the book of Psalms, we will see that David did not shy away from such issues. There is a lot to learn from David:

- His reaction to Goliath (1 Sam 17:26).
- His reaction when Bathsheba's first child whom he had been praying about died (2 Sam 12:20).
- His reaction when the prophet convicted him of his sin (2 Sam 12: 1–14).
- His heart to give (2 Sam 24:24).
- His reaction even after lamenting—he never forgot to refocus on God and praise His name (See the book of Psalms).

One of the beauties of prayer is that you do not have to hide or run away from your Father in the face of adversity, pain, failures, mistakes or unexpected tragedies. It might be tough, and you will feel the pain, but the comfort of knowing that God is with you and that His peace is with you, is priceless.

REFLECTION

1. What is that painful situation you are probably angry about because you feel God failed you?
2. Can you let it out either in writing or speech and express how you feel to the Father? (Even though you break down in tears or you feel like wailing, express yourself to your Father without holding back. Be still and ask Him to comfort you and speak to you. This may play out in different forms. Some people might hear a voice, and some might not hear anything. Some people might have a witness in their spirit while some others might feel a comforting atmosphere. Just believe He heard you and will comfort you).
3. Write down this experience.
4. Think about the great things God has done for you and just bask in the thoughts.

IV

Jesus, Our Intercessor and Ultimate Prayer Model

"

Jesus prayed about everything, in every situation and place.

"

One day, I was having a conversation with God in my mind about my worries, confusion and anxiety, and He told me clearly and firmly, "Relax, Jesus is your standard. Read and study how he handled fame, success and exploits to finish well and not derail. Learn from people, leaders and fathers, but never forget that Jesus is the ultimate model and standard."

Afterwards, I started to study the life of Jesus. Interestingly, you can never finish this study because the more you seek, the more you want to know. With knowing Jesus or walking with God, we never "arrive", we keep learning.

A few things interest me about the prayer life of Jesus: First, He made out time to fellowship with the Father and pray, though He and God are one. The Bible even states that He went early to pray as it was His custom (Luke 5:16; 22:39–41). For spontaneous people like me, we need to set aside time just to pray and fellowship with God. This creates the discipline to be devoted to God and walk with Him. It helps our maturity and creates memories and a history with God—it is a beautiful experience. For me, it was a tall order—I do not like routines. I like to "reinvent the wheel", but I learnt that I needed to have a routine to grow and become more intimate with Him. It has been a process for me and when I am unable to pray at a set time, I make up for it by staying in fellowship with God all day. I pray to stay connected and remain conscious that I house God, and He is in me. This consciousness changes everything. I learnt this from Jesus. Remember that He came and lived as a man, tapping into the same supernatural resources available to us today.

Secondly, Jesus prayed about everything, in every situation and place. He was a typical example of a man of prayer. He did this effortlessly, spending long hours, deep in prayer; therefore, teaching us the necessity of spending quality time in fellowship with God. There is also a place for saying short prayers; Jesus made declarations and said short prayers that impacted lives greatly and changed situations. At times, we are faced with situations where we need to exert our authority and make declarations. Even if we speak few words, we should expect results. For instance, He showed us how to deal with the devil, the accuser, in Matthew 4:1–11 by engaging him with the word of God:

1 Then was Jesus led up of the Spirit into the wilderness to be tempted of the devil.
2 And when he had fasted forty days and forty nights, he was afterward an hungred.
3 And when the tempter came to him, he said, if thou be the Son of God, command that these stones be made bread.
4 But he answered and said, it is written, Man shall not live by bread alone, but by every word that proceedeth out of the mouth of God.
5 Then the devil taketh him up into the holy city, and setteth him on a pinnacle of the temple,
6 And saith unto him, if thou be the Son of God, cast thyself down: for it is written, He shall give his angels charge concerning thee: and in their hands they shall bear thee up, lest at any time thou dash thy foot against a stone.
7 Jesus said unto him, it is written again, thou shalt not tempt the Lord thy God.
8 Again, the devil taketh him up into an exceeding high mountain, and sheweth him all the kingdoms of the world, and the glory of them;

9 And saith unto him, all these things will I give thee, if thou wilt fall down and worship me.
10 Then saith Jesus unto him, get thee hence, Satan: for it is written, Thou shalt worship the Lord thy God, and him only shalt thou serve.
11 Then the devil leaveth him, and, behold, angels came and ministered unto him.

Just as it was written in James 4:7, subject yourself to God, resist the devil and he will flee from you. Jesus subjected himself to God. He did nothing without God; therefore, it was no surprise that He was able to resist the devil and rebuke the storm. "So the men marvelled, saying, 'Who can this be, that even the winds and the sea obey Him?'" (Matthew 8:27).

He thanked God for things He was yet to receive because He believed that when He prayed, His father heard Him. He exuded so much confidence and trust in God and showed us the posture to maintain when we pray. An example was when He prayed before feeding the five thousand:

13 When Jesus heard it, He departed from there by boat to a deserted place by Himself. But when the multitudes heard it, they followed Him on foot from the cities.

14 And when Jesus went out, He saw a great multitude; and He was moved with compassion for them and healed their sick.
15 When it was evening, His disciples came to Him, saying, "This is a deserted place, and the hour is already late. Send the multitudes away, that they may go into the villages and buy themselves food."
16 But Jesus said to them, "They do not need to go away. You give them something to eat."
17 And they said to Him, "We have here only five loaves and two fish."
18 He said, "Bring them here to Me."
19 Then He commanded the multitudes to sit down on the grass. And He took the five loaves and the two fish, and looking up to heaven, He blessed and broke and gave the loaves to the disciples; and the disciples gave to the multitudes.
20 So they all ate and were filled, and they took up twelve baskets full of the fragments that remained.
21 Now those who had eaten were about five thousand men, besides women and children. (Matthew 14:13–21).

He prayed in solitude (Mark 1:35), "Now in the morning, having risen a long while before daylight, He went out and departed to a solitary place; and there He prayed." He prayed in public and in the synagogue. He prayed in His own words and sang the Psalms. Till His last breath, He prayed and communicated with His father. "He went a little farther and fell on His face, and prayed, saying, 'O My Father, if it is possible, let this cup pass from Me; nevertheless, not as I will, but as You will'" (Matthew 26:39).

I love the fact that the Bible includes the time Jesus went to Gethsemane to pray and fellowship with God just before He went to the cross. It showed His struggle; the pressure that came with His purpose—the pain, the contemplation and ultimately, He surrendered to His Father's will. I am grateful that this portion was not omitted from the Bible, because it teaches us that the place of prayer is a place of strengthening, conviction and surrender.

I cannot count the number of times I have found myself at my own "Mount of Gethsemane" relinquishing my pain (sometimes in doubt); asking God if what I was about to do was the only way, asking for other ways, and sometimes suggesting options. In these moments, I have learnt to surrender my will for the Father's will to be done. It might be painful, long and daunting but at the end, it will be worth it. Just imagine if Jesus had not done the will of God, we would not have life as we know it; we would not have the privilege to cry out, "Abba Father" or enjoy the benefits of sonship.

Let me encourage you, please do not bail out of your assignment. If you feel tired and worn out, you can express how you feel to God. Stay in His presence and fellowship with Him, and you will find the strength to go on. Intimacy with God, which is often fuelled by fellowship, empowers you to surrender, especially now that we have the Holy Spirit. Do not ever feel that God does not understand. I love the way Hebrews 12:1–5, The Message, puts it. Go over what He went through, view your own journey in that light, and you will be encouraged.

> 1-3 Do you see what this means—all these pioneers who blazed the way, all these veterans cheering us on? It means we'd better get on with it. Strip down, start running—and never quit! No extra spiritual fat, no parasitic sins. Keep your eyes on Jesus, who both began and finished this race we're in. Study how he did it. Because he never lost sight of where he was headed—that exhilarating finish in and with God—he could put up with anything along the way: Cross,

shame, whatever. And now he's there, in the place of honor, right alongside God. When you find yourselves flagging in your faith, go over that story again, item by item, that long litany of hostility he plowed through. That will shoot adrenaline into your souls!

4-11 In this all-out match against sin, others have suffered far worse than you, to say nothing of what Jesus went through—all that bloodshed! So, don't feel sorry for yourselves. Or have you forgotten how good parents treat children, and that God regards you as his children?

My dear child, don't shrug off God's discipline, but don't be crushed by it either. It's the child he loves that he disciplines; the child he embraces, he also corrects.

God is educating you; that's why you must never drop out. He's treating you as dear children. This trouble you're in isn't punishment; it's training, the normal experience of children. Only irresponsible parents leave children to fend for themselves. Would you prefer an irresponsible God? We respect our own parents for training and not spoiling us, so why not embrace God's training so we can truly live?

You see why we cannot joke with having an effective prayer life with God, the kind that is built on fellowship and intimacy? There will be days when words may fail you, but the Holy Spirit is ever present, making intercessions for you because Jesus is still interceding for us to this day.

The more you grow in God, the more you realise that prayer is not selfish. You begin to move from praying for "you and yours" to praying for the heart of the Father and not for vanity, but for a desire to please God. The more He reveals His heart to you, the more you are drawn in and endeared to Him. You begin to see and understand His will, His desire for mankind, His love for souls, His interpretation of the Kingdom, and His wish to reveal heaven here on earth. Your prayer begins to move from "needs" to "impact" such that even when you are tired and weak, you are strengthened by the fact that you are in the centre of His will to birth something bigger than you.

Think about it, what made Jesus say to God, "Not my will but yours"? I am sure that He peeped into the future through the eyes of God. He saw you and me, and He knew that we were worth it. The day my eyes caught the depth of the prayer in John 17, I cried my eyes out because I saw the heart of a lover. I met with the Father who loved me enough and made provision for me even before I was born. I saw what it meant to be an intercessor, I saw the higher calling of prayer, and I understood that it was not about me. Right there, I made a commitment to spend the rest of my life with God. When it comes to my Saviour, nothing is more important, nothing else matters, time cannot confine me because no time is too much to spend with Him. Prayer is an invitation to intimacy and fellowship. It is not a routine or punishment or task. Even on the days when it feels long and tiring, the thought of Him praying over me and interceding for me concerning things I probably will never know about just makes me cry out, "Abba Father, thank you, I love you", and gives me strength to remain in His presence and carry Him everywhere I go.

Just like Jesus, I have learnt that wherever I am is an altar and I am forever connected to Him because He is in me and I in Him, John 15. When you understand this, you will stop struggling to pray, you will not have to wait for a song to play before you worship, you will not have to mutter words before you can connect to Him or always start your prayer in tongues before you can connect to Him. It will not matter how long you have spent or what the demands are to spend time in His presence.

With this reality, I can understand the scripture that says I am never alone. He is with me all the time. If a situation comes up on the spot for me to tackle, I do not have to run to anyone to pray for me before I tackle it, neither do I need to take permission from my boss to go home and pray. I can create an altar of prayer right there because I am a mobile altar. I just need to engage the spirit of God within me. I can say a short prayer under my breath, but I must believe that I will receive direction from God on what to do for such battles that have to be won immediately. To clarify, it is not bad to send a message to a friend, pastor or community to join you in prayers as long as you are doing it based on the principle of agreement and not because you do not believe you can pray and get results. For this reason, we must learn the following from Jesus:

- We always need to build up our prayer reserve because we do not know when we will need to draw strength to handle unforeseen situations, which will require immediate action. In these moments, declaring a fast and praying for hours is not an option. For instance, when Jesus had to rebuke the storm or how he responded to the Pharisees' spontaneous trick questions.

23 Now when He got into a boat, His disciples followed Him.

24 And suddenly a great tempest arose on the sea, so that the boat was covered with the waves. But He was asleep.
25 Then His disciples came to Him and awoke Him, saying, "Lord, save us! We are perishing!"
26 But He said to them, "Why are you fearful, O you of little faith?" Then He arose and rebuked the winds and the sea, and there was a great calm.
27 So the men marvelled, saying, "Who can this be, that even the winds and the sea obey Him?" (Matthew 8:23–27).

- You cannot pray effectively if you do not know the Word of God and if the Word is not rooted in you. The Word affects your faith which in turn impacts your prayer. Remember, faith comes by hearing and hearing by the Word of God, Romans 10:17, and it is the prayer of faith that is answered. Aside from praying to God to help your unbelief, get into the Word.
- You cannot pray effectively if you do not know who you are, understand your authority, exercise this identity and expect results.

- If you lack an intimate relationship with God, which may occur because you have not invested time to fellowship with God, it will affect your prayer life. Prayer becomes a routine, and you will become aggravated because you do not know the will of the Father.
- It is important to pray for the will of the Father and you can only know this through intimacy with Him.
- How long should you pray? I believe Jesus showed us that it varies. He had scheduled times when He prayed and fellowshipped with God for a lengthy time. He had moments where He declared God's Word. There were times when He engaged in short prayers, gave commands, and there were results. He prayed silently and loudly. Sometimes He was groaning and at other times, He simply rebuked the devil (See Matthew 26:36–46, Hebrews 5:7, Mark 4:35–41).

I believe as we grow, it is imperative that we grow into all of these. It is important to have scheduled times to pray while remaining spontaneous to pray-as-led and to cultivate a relationship with God where He can interrupt our schedule. It takes discipline to have an effective prayer life. Ultimately, we must learn to spend quality time in prayer. There is a demand for that.

Jesus encouraged us to pray always and not give up regardless of the situation (Luke 18:1). Also, we should not only pray about spiritual things and decide that our career is off limits for prayers or scrutiny from God. God is interested in every aspect of our lives. Do not put God in a box. Proverbs 3:6 says, "In all your ways acknowledge Him, And He shall direct your paths."

Jesus was an excellent intercessor. He interceded more than he prayed for personal things. It is not bad to pray for personal needs but pray for Kingdom matters as well. It is either he was praying for the blind to see or for provision to feed the hungry or raising the dead. There are many things happening around us and God is looking for intercessors to birth the revival of transformation and mirror heaven on earth. There needs to be more to prayer than "what will I eat, drink and where I will live?" God has explained this in Matthew 6:24–33. In fact, in Matthew 6:33, we were told how to live and what our priority should be: "But seek first the kingdom of God and His righteousness, and all these things shall be added to you."

1 Thessalonian 5:16–18 admonishes us to "pray without ceasing". You may be wondering, how do I pray without ceasing? Jesus did. This does not mean that you would not do other things, it just means that you will pray consistently and be conscious of God at all times. In between our schedule, we ought to seek God, say short prayers, stay connected to Him and intercede for people as the need arises. We are communing with Him like we would with our friends; we are into each other, which is a beautiful experience. God wants you and me, but He is not forceful. The onus is on us to make prayer a lifestyle.

One of the aspects I love about living a prayerful life is that I can just stop to say, "Thank you Jesus" over and over. Sometimes, I lose my peace or my heart is pounding in anxiety and I cannot tell why. I just pray. Most times, in situations like this, I pray in the Holy Ghost. I know I have prayed through when I sense that my peace is restored. Sometimes, days later, I might hear the testimony of someone who had a miraculous intervention at the same time I was led to pray or shortly after, but there are other times that I never find out why I was led to pray and that is fine.

Therefore, it is possible to pray without ceasing when you understand that prayer is more of a lifestyle than a routine, which Jesus exemplified so well. Also, the Bible says that Jesus grew in wisdom and favour; therefore, if He needed to grow, then we need to embrace growth as well. With God we cannot remain the same. The same is applicable to our prayer lives. You should not remain on the same level. The prayer of Jesus for us in John 17 is a must read:

> Jesus spoke these words, lifted up His eyes to heaven, and said: "Father, the hour has come. Glorify Your Son, that Your Son also may glorify You, as You have given Him authority over all flesh, that He should give eternal life to as many as You have given Him. And this is eternal life, that they may know You, the only true God, and Jesus Christ whom You have sent. I have glorified You on the earth. I have finished the work which You have given Me to do. And now, O Father, glorify Me together with Yourself, with the glory which I had with You before the world was.

Jesus prays for his disciples:

"I have manifested Your name to the men whom You have given Me out of the world. They were Yours, You gave them to Me, and they have kept Your word. Now they have known that all things which You have given Me are from You. For I have given to them the words which You have given Me; and they have received them, and have known surely that I came forth from You; and they have believed that You sent Me.

I pray for them. I do not pray for the world but for those whom You have given Me, for they are Yours. And all Mine are Yours, and Yours are Mine, and I am glorified in them. Now I am no longer in the world, but these are in the world, and I come to You. Holy Father, keep through Your name those whom You have given Me, that they may be one as We are. While I was with them in the world, I kept them in Your name. Those whom You gave Me I have kept; and none of them is lost except the son of perdition, that the Scripture might be fulfilled. But now I come to You, and these things I speak in the world, that they may have My joy fulfilled in themselves. I have given them Your word; and the world has hated them because they are not of the world, just as I am not of the world. I do not pray that You should take them out of the world, but that You should keep them from the evil one. They are not of the world, just as I am not of the world. Sanctify them by Your truth. Your word is truth. As You sent Me into the world, I also have sent them into the world. And for their sakes I sanctify Myself, that they also may be sanctified by the truth.

Jesus prays for all believers:

"I do not pray for these alone, but also for those who will believe in Me through their word; that they all may be one, as You, Father, are in Me, and I in You; that they also may be one in Us, that the world may believe that You sent Me. And the glory which You gave Me I have given them, that they may be one just as We are one: I in them, and You in Me; that they may be made perfect in one, and that the world may know that You have sent Me, and have loved them as You have loved Me.

Father, I desire that they also whom You gave Me may be with Me where I am, that they may behold My glory which You have given Me; for You loved Me before the foundation of the world. O righteous Father! The world has not known You, but I have known You; and these have known that You sent Me. And I have declared to them Your name, and will declare it, that the love with which You loved Me may be in them, and I in them."

REFLECTION

1. Do you know Jesus as your Lord and personal saviour or have you walked away from your relationship with Him? Is all you know about Jesus Christ hearsay? If that is the case, do you desire to know Him for yourself and accept Him as your Lord and personal saviour or are you ready to rededicate your life to Christ?
2. Do you need to make a commitment to put basic structures in place for your prayer life? If the answer is yes, I advise that you start with achievable goals and grow from there. Do not say you will pray for one hour at 4 a.m. daily, because everyone makes it sound like that is the minimum requirement; rather, start with what is achievable, be consistent, then grow from there. Stretch yourself a bit, measure yourself and keep growing. Also note the routine you create. If you find yourself lagging, remember God is your Father and you can approach Him outside any regimented timeline. Talk to Him, ask for strength and help and keep moving. God does not correct with condemnation. He

might convict with love, but He will never condemn you.

3. You cannot pray effectively without God. Fellowship, intimacy and love should always guide you.
4. List your top ten friends or the top two communities that you belong to. Do they have the same goals as you do as regards growing in prayer? This is very important because you need friends and communities that aid your growth.

V

We Have Work to Do

"

Intercession is not just casually **mentioning people's names** and getting bored after five minutes.

"

> So, he answered and said to me: "This is the word of the Lord to Zerubbabel: 'Not by might nor by power, but by My Spirit,' Says the Lord of hosts."
>
> – Zechariah 4:6.

I love the fact that we do not need to rely on our strength all the time. We should realise that we are in a covenant relationship with God and we have our part to play. We have work to do, and it is important that you do not get overwhelmed by the amount of work to be done. Therefore, start small and grow gradually, taking one step at a time.

Going Beyond Yourself: Intercession

People often ask:

"Imisi, I want to pray, how do I go about it?"

"What do I pray about?"

"It feels like the longest I can pray is five minutes. What do I do?"

"If you start by praying genuinely for different countries, their governments, your family, the wounded, the broken, the orphans, war-torn nations, refugees, the body of Christ, lost souls, and so on, you won't be done in a year." So I tell them, rather, to start by interceding for others.

There is a lot to pray about. There are inventions locked up in heaven that we need here on earth, but who is praying about them? There are countries who have not heard the gospel, but who is praying about them?

In the past, whenever I scrolled through my Instagram feed and found a picture of a celebrity who is not saved, my initial response (while shaking my head) would be, "Oh Lord save them", or if the picture was indecent, my response would be, "Na wa oo, God you are patient gan o. Lord save them."

One day, I was spending time with God and He brought my attention to my "holy" statement and said: "Daughter, who is praying for the souls of these people? Don't you know I love them too and I do not desire any soul to perish? Who is genuinely interceding for them? Just imagine what

I can do with them, imagine the souls that could be won through them, imagine them in a true relationship with me, just imagine. The next time you see pictures like that, change your irritation to compassion and pray for them. Praying for them has nothing to do with them posting their pictures on social media."

This hit home because I remembered that God gave me some privileged information in 2008 to pray for certain celebrities. They were three. Two of them died, and I cried when I heard of their deaths because I knew I did not intercede as I should. I am not saying it was my prayer that would have saved them, but I knew that God had a reason for telling me about it. Whether they gave their lives to Christ before dying is still a mystery. God is a merciful God and He probably raised other intercessors because He will not force anyone to accept Him, neither will He force them to intercede for anyone. I repented in tears and asked God to forgive me.

Intercession is not just casually mentioning people's names and getting bored after five minutes. You know how you get when the prayer is personal? You know how you fast, pray, raise prayer requests amongst friends and pastors when you are waiting on a miracle? You know that feeling of passion, hope and consistency? We need to get that way when it comes to intercession. When it comes to praying for a matter that is distant from us or does not impact us directly, we need to get as passionate and dedicated as we would be if it were to be our personal request. I pray that we can catch the depth and importance of intercession to the Father's heart.

Intercession is one of the most ignored aspects of prayer because it takes a lot of sacrifice, usually unnoticed by men but noticed by God. While many of us want to feel cool and get recognition from the men that we are interceding for, at times, you might not see the outcome of the prayer in your lifetime, but your intercession would have paved the way for generations unborn.

Imagine if you were told by God to pray for James in Australia, and you do not know this person, and may never meet him. In fact, you might not even be the person that will lead him to Christ. It is easy to neglect these prayers, forgetting that your orders are from God. However, if He asks you to pray for something or someone specific, you should do so wholeheartedly, for God is our rewarder and not man.

One of the people I admire greatly when it comes to engaging the principles of intercession and focusing on Kingdom based prayers is Bishop David Oyedepo. I have heard him say in different sermons how he signed up to live by Matthew 6:33, and how God is constantly adding "every other thing" to his life. He spends his time praying for souls, praying kingdom expansion prayers, going out to evangelise and so on. You cannot put God first and regret it. This reward is not limited to material blessings but much more. Today, we see God do incredible things through Bishop Oyedepo; we see history being made with him, and he is never shy to tell us that Matthew 6:33 is the secret to his success.

Another story that fires me up is one I saw in *The God's Generals – The Revivalist Edition* by Roberts Liardon. A group of people came together in August 1727 – twenty-four men and twenty-four women convened – to pray round the clock; different people taking shifts per hour to pray about anything God put in their minds, but mostly for revival and the spread of the gospel across the world. It was documented that this prayer chain lasted for a hundred years. That is incredible! One century to pray for whatever was in God's heart, especially for revival and the propagation of the gospel. This was the womb that birthed several revivals across the world. I believe we are beneficiaries of the answers to such prayers.

Please let us process this properly. They did not have technology as we have it today – social media, conference calls, live videos – so it was not a walk in the park. Just imagine how much they would have achieved if they had all the privileges we have today. We should ask ourselves: Can we secure the next one hundred years for the Lord? Can we pray the manifestation of Isaiah 60 over our lives, our children and unborn generations? We just cannot be consumed by our individual lives, there is a generation unborn depending on our prayers.

So where do you start from? That's easy, we will start with the last thing God told you. Maybe you are thinking, "Imisi, I don't even know the last thing God said to me." Do not worry, get your Bible, open it and you will find a thousand and one things to pray about. At times, we are so focused on hearing or seeing spectacular things that we miss out on what God is doing now. Thank God for the Bible, it contains a lot of things God is saying. It is the written Word of God. Let us start from there.

Here is a list of things to pray about:

- Pray for souls.
- Pray for your leaders and government.
- Pray concerning your assignment.
- Pray for the body of Christ.
- Pray for missionaries.
- Pray for the nations of the earth.

Peradventure, you have a situation that you have been interceding for years, please do not give up. Keep praying and thanking God for a glorious outcome. My extended family and I have been praying concerning a situation for over eighteen years and we are still praying. There is no day that we do not cry, wonder and ask questions, but repeatedly, we get God's assurance and hope, so we are encouraged to keep praying and trusting. Be encouraged.

Learning How to Steward Your Joy and Using It as a Weapon in Prayer

"Therefore, with joy will you draw water from the wells of salvation" (Isaiah 12:3). Remember that salvation is God's redemptive plan to reconcile us to Himself by the sacrifice of His only begotten son who shed His blood for our cleansing. But guess what? Redemption is just one of the benefits of salvation, and the way to draw from the wells of salvation is with joy.

I love this passage: "Then he said to them, go your way, eat the fat, drink the sweet, and send portions to those for whom nothing is prepared; for this day is holy to our Lord. Do not sorrow, for the joy of the Lord is your strength" (Nehemiah 8:10). To live victoriously whilst waiting to see the outcome of your prayers, you need to learn how to steward your joy. You need to understand the force of joy. I chose the word steward deliberately. Let us examine what stewardship means. According to dictionary.com, it means, "The responsible overseeing and protection of something considered worth caring for and preserving, or the job of supervising or taking care of something, such as an organisation or property."

I love the above definition because it highlights a few things that cover what I have in mind about stewarding our joy. Note the words: "Worth caring for and preserving". I love the fact that this definition gives room to say that it is our job to supervise, protect and oversee what we consider worth caring for and preserving. Trust me, our joy is worth much more. Even Jesus endured the cross for the joy set ahead of Him (Hebrews 12:1–3).

As I prepared for a ministration a while back, God highlighted the picture of an egg and we got into a conversation. God said, "Imisi, if you had a bowl filled with eggs to carry, how would you handle it and how would it impact the way you walked?" I responded, "I would carry it carefully and protect it from falling or breaking." Then I thought about the fact that when I go grocery shopping, I pay more attention to how I carry and position the eggs in the car. If I tossed the other bags into the boot, I would not toss the bag with the eggs.

Then He said, "Beautiful, treat your joy that way. Be conscious and careful about your joy. Learn to steward your joy, it is an infallible weapon and asset. The same way you are careful so the egg does not crack, be careful so you do not break your joy. Imagine if you are going for an event, and you were holding the egg, you would not want it to break, especially because of the smell. Fight for your joy, a believer's life without joy is open to foul spirits."

To further prove this, one time, on our way to an event, we had to stop at a store to buy eggs, the moment we entered the car, the people seated by the person holding the eggs were careful not to tip the crate over or hit an egg. So imagine, if we can treat a mere food item this way, how much more for our eternal value? This is vital, especially when we are expecting our miracles and even maintaining a miracle, we need joy.

Practicing the following things have helped me and I believe they will help you too:

- Focus on the character of God, e.g. the goodness of God. No matter what happens, God is good; He can be trusted. He loves me and hears me when I pray.
- Believe in God's sovereignty because nothing takes Him by surprise.
- Choose to remember the things God did in times past both big and small. I wrote in one of my Psalms: "Do not belittle the big miracles of yesterday because of challenges of today". God wiped out an entire generation because they chose to forget His goodness and murmured (Numbers 14:26–31). I believe you cannot meditate on the faithfulness of God and murmur at the same time. Even if you are tempted to complain, you are so full of gratitude that it swallows up the murmuring.

- Find reasons to be thankful. "Thank you Lord for the weather, thank you for provision to eat out, thank you for safety." I remember the praise party I had in my house the day I found my sister's wedding ring, which had earlier gone missing in my care and I had searched for days. That act encouraged someone else who heard the testimony. She did not understand why I was so joyful about a mere ring when there were other pressing matters. She was really encouraged. My thought was: if He did this one, what then can't He do? He pays attention to my little unspoken requests, how much more the expressed ones? If you create a culture of thanksgiving, before you know it, you will always have a reason to be joyful.
- See things God's way: Fight for your joy by choosing to see things the way God sees them. It changes your perspective.
- Steward your promises through the word: I make sure I feed on the word of God and steward my promises by writing down my prophecies. I write almost every day to God. I recently started recording my prophecies when I can and listening to them repeatedly.

I do the same with messages and materials that help build my joy.

- Develop phrases from God's word: Over the years, I have developed phrases based on the word to jolt me back when I feel down or see traces of sadness in my life. For example, "This too shall pass, it's only a process", "I am loved by God", "If he did not spare His only begotten son to die for me, what then will He withhold from me?", "No devil! Not today or tomorrow or the future, God has got me".
- Testify for the future: I testify in advance in front of the mirror or in my room or before my husband.
- Meditate on God's word: I meditate on the goodness of God.
- Celebrate God: I laugh, dance or deliberately worship God despite how I feel. I have engaged in laughing and dancing when I was crying and in pain but as I kept at it, it became real and before I knew it, I was engrossed in it.
- Pray: I pray in the Holy Ghost.
- Fellowship with others: I speak with some of my covenant friends who don't fail to

remind me of the promises of God over my life. We could just decide to have a praise chant over the phone.

Please note, these are not theologies or doctrines, but practical ways I have been able to maintain my joy. I have heard other men of God and Christians use some of the examples and it worked for them; however, this is not cast in stone. Feel free to ask the Holy Spirit to reveal what to do because that is one sure way to maintain your joy.

The Force of Testimony

"We overcame by the blood of the lamb and the words of our testimony" (Revelation 12:11).

This is a powerful force that jolts our confidence in God when we pray. It is like reminding God of what He did once, because God is not a respecter of persons. What He did for one, He will do for another. I celebrate testimonies of others and testify in advance. I have written my testimonies in advance and continually use them as my prayer points. God has reproduced in my life, certain testimonies I keyed into through prayers, seeds or thanksgiving.

Sometime ago, a friend of mine shared a testimony where she was blessed with one thousand, five hundred dollars. I was so excited, and I prayed the same over my life especially because I had an upcoming trip. I prayed for three thousand, five hundred dollars. I later discovered that her faith was inspired by a testimony she heard from an online course we were taking together called Kingdom Culture by Bethel Church. At the end of my trip, when I calculated all the funds I had received and spent, it was about three thousand, five hundred dollars, minus other gift items.

This encouraged my faith in prayer and the force of testimonies. I do not joke with testimonies. I recount them when praying and thank God for mine. I cannot count how many times I speak to myself in a day, how many times I imagine my miracles and how I will share the testimony. It is beautiful and empowering. It makes prayer powerful.

In 2017, I met an amazing lady and we became close friends. I realised that God had a way of supernaturally providing for her events on a large scale. The ministry I am privileged to lead was also coming into a new season of expansion and I was not sure how it would happen. So, I listened to my friend's testimony repeatedly, and I prayed over the ministry and sowed a seed. She prayed with me and I kept stewarding her testimony. She had an unusual testimony of ease when it came to financing projects for the ministry. The rest they say, is history. We made two major moves between November 2017 and May 2018, and God blew my mind. He exceeded our expectations and we are more confident to take the next major steps ahead of us, rest assured that if He did it before, He will do it again.

How Do You Stay "Prayed Up" (Being in a Consistent Place of Prayer)?

In each chapter, I have added few suggestions on how to stay prayed up based on the principle we found in the life of Jesus that prayer is more of a lifestyle than an activity on our to do list. If you maintain a close relationship with God by having constant fellowship that breeds intimacy, you will be prayed up, thus making the scripture, "pray without ceasing", a reality. Aside from being a devout student of the Bible, I will recommend the following:

Create the right environment: A while back, I travelled to minister in Geneva. The host of the event and I stayed in an apartment belonging to an amazing lady. All through my stay, I literally saw a scripture everywhere. It was a beautiful sight and an experience I have not forgotten. She had scriptures on the walls; the password for the Wi-Fi was a mixture of scriptures and letters, even down to the cookie jar, which had a beautiful inscription that said: "Taste and see that the Lord is good". The environment drew me to God, whose presence was strong. It was not just aesthetics – if you pray well and long enough in a place, you will be able to tell this – the Spirit of God was there. Therefore, create an environment that enables you to pray like my host who pasted scriptures everywhere. Even if I was not a Christian, I would have been aware that there was a God living in that apartment.

Pay attention to the kind of music you listen to: I started scrutinising the lyrics of the gospel songs I listen to and I observed that some were not Biblical at all, they did not edify. I have personal check points to evaluate the impact of a song in my life. I ask myself whether the song is edifying? If it glorifies the flesh or makes me more aware of my identity in Christ? If it is encouraging/soothing? What impact does it leave on me?

8 Finally, brethren, whatever things are true, whatever things are noble, whatever things are just, whatever things are pure, whatever things are lovely, whatever things are of good report, if there is any virtue and if there is anything praiseworthy—meditate on these things.
9 The things which you learned and received and heard and saw in me, these do, and the God of peace will be with you (Philippians 4:8).

Pay attention to the company you keep: Even though the disciples of Jesus slept off when he took them to pray alongside Him on the mountain, you will agree with me that praying was not strange to them and Jesus was showing us the importance of belonging to a community that prays. Little wonder in Acts 1 that Jesus could instruct them to wait as a community in the upper room. It is important to have friends that believe in prayer. Pray effectively and desire to grow in the Lord as well.

Often, people genuinely want to grow in their faith and prayer life but keep close friends that do not have the same goals—I am talking about core friends. Jesus had disciples. He led a large crowd, but did not take the crowd to Gethsemane or reappeared to the crowd after ressurrection. While we are in the world, we are not of the world. We will meet people of different faiths and we must love them, but we cannot be equally yoked with them or compromise on godly standards all in the name of loving them or being friends with them. Remember, 1 Corinthians 5:33, says, "Bad company corrupts good manners".

"Do not be unequally yoked together with unbelievers. For what fellowship has righteousness with lawlessness? And what communion has light with darkness?" (2 Corinthians 6:14 New King James Version).

This is one of the ideas behind one of our platforms, #WhenFriendsPray. It is where true friendship is built while offering undiluted worship and prayers to God. I tell people: "You don't have friends? Attend. You have friends? Attend. There is room for you." The ministry did not start with all of us being the best of friends, but today we are covenant friends. We are one family and we are consciously building a community devoted to daily propagating the revival of true worship, and the transformation of lives and nations while sustaining healthy relationships. Please pay attention to the company you keep.

Embrace personal development: When it comes to your relationship with God, you have to work out your salvation with fear and trembling (Philippians 2:12). You need to take personal responsibility for your growth in the Lord. If you want to pray more, take responsibility. If you want to serve better, take responsibility. If you want to intercede more, take responsibility. Desiring to pray effectively, to hear God clearly, or to do mighty things for God without taking responsibility is like a student wishing to get top results in an exam without studying or preparing. I love the saying, "While we are waiting for God to move, God is waiting on us to move." These are some ideas on how to invest in your personal development:

- Plan to fellowship with God: I take out time to pray and fellowship with God. Therefore, if you want to have a date night with your spouse, you need to plan towards it, that is, reserve the time, place and so on. This does not stop other affectionate moments throughout the rest of the day. It's just that we have stipulated time in our day, solely for us, no distractions, no interference. That's how I see setting prayer altars and routines with God. I set the alarm on my phone to remind me in case I forget. I had to because there was a time I was so forgetful that I had to set an alarm to remind me to eat. So I thought: "Why not set a reminder to feed myself spiritually too?"

- Study the Bible: I recommend studying the Bible for yourself. Know the scriptures. Study the life of Jesus repeatedly.
- Read Christian literature: I read a lot of Christian literature, because I can see it is Christian by the way it aligns with the word. If it does not, I push it aside. I read authors I believe have been proven over time as authorities and those that I believe are profound even if they aren't popular.
- Listen to sermons: I listen to a lot of sermons. There was a season in my life when I would listen to a minimum of four or five at a go. Little did I know I would depend on this reservoir later, especially in seasons where I could barely catch my breath.
- Get an accountability partner: I am accountable to different people based on my relationship with them. I have peer to peer accountability partners; I have slightly older accountability partners; I have father-

daughter accountability partners, and I have a spiritual Father. I have pastors and leaders in my life. God has blessed me with an amazing support system, which I was wise enough to build over the years with Him leading. Learn how to manage access, it will help you a lot.

- Be disciplined: I discipline myself to pray in the Holy Ghost as often as possible.
- Celebrate: Celebrate your present level in God even as you desire the next.

Make History with God, Be Adventurous, Take Risks and Be Obedient

Have you ever run out of the house stark naked because you were late to work? I guess your answer is the same as mine – No. This was a scenario God showed me one day. No matter how late you are, you make out time to get dressed. God said, "Make time for me Imisi, you make time for the things that are important to you." Make history with God, obey Him instantly, take risks and be adventurous within the limits of righteousness.

Talking about being adventurous and taking risks, in 2017, we had our last event for the year, and I heard the Lord say to me to raise a twenty-four-hour prayer altar, which we did. We had different people taking different shifts per hour. It was an exciting experience, different from what we tried to do in 2006.

In February 2018, God said, "Have the twenty-four hours prayer online as opposed to people praying alone." In other words, we were all supposed to pray for twenty-four hours, but this time online, so at any time when anyone logs in, someone is praying. While some could take hourly shifts, some others knew they were going to have to pray all through. We obeyed this instruction with the resources we had, and it was good. I had a ministration in between, took a few breaks, and then continued. The next event we had after the prayers was not like anything we had ever seen.

In May 2018, we started the school of intercession and God instructed me that we had the twenty-four hours of prayer online again and we had people join us from different parts of the world. This time around, I prayed for twenty hours at a stretch. It was amazing and I was on fire. I had a series of encounters—people were logged on for hours and we had more people join in. It was yet another adventure in God, and that week I started seeing miracles happen. Above all, my mind was renewed. It was so beautiful, and we prayed from the book of Ephesians throughout. I am bracing up for the next one.

This adventure has opened many people up to the possibility of praying for twenty-four hours, not so that we can brag about it, but to practice obedience to God. You never can tell what your obedience will birth and how it will impact others.

I have been mulling over this book in my heart for a while, but I never saw it coming this year. Under the inspiration of the Holy Ghost, I took the risk of writing it; ninety-five per cent of which was written in less than forty-eight hours, and the whole book was written in less than four days. There is no way I could have achieved that on my own without His help and grace. I did not have a sketch before now; it all came and happened in time because I said YES! I accepted the invitation to take a risk and go on an adventure with Him. Now I am more stretched than I was before, and I had incredible encounters while writing this book. I am excited and ready for yet another adventure in Him.

The more you seek God, the more intriguing you will find Him, and the more He will stretch you. This makes prayer beautiful.

VI

Prayer Looks Good on You

"

Accept the invitation to fellowship and **pray today** and ensure you have fun while at it. . .

"

I believe strongly that prayer is an invitation to fellowship with God, which breeds intimacy and powers our confidence in approaching Him. It is an invitation to share our burdens, receive strength, get equipped, intercede for others, birth ideas and trigger transformation in the lives of individuals and nations around us. It grants us access to the provision, wealth and dominion available to us. It helps and positions us to birth heaven on earth. It has been my place of power, strength, comfort, victory, warfare and communion.

There is this beauty and radiance that emanates from you; this beauty cannot be ascribed to any product. This beauty, aura and presence comes from spending time with God. It is so nourishing to the spirit and soul. Prayer looks good on us all if we embrace His invitation to keep growing. I would not want to end this book without mentioning this: *what do we do with unanswered prayers?*

I do not claim to be an expert or have all the answers when it comes to prayer, but I do know one thing – I go back to God when I do not see the answers I desire, especially the ones I am convinced I got an assurance about. Amid the emotions, pain and disappointments, I am driven back to God and not away from Him. I approach Him as my Father and a sovereign God who cannot be questioned. I accept that maybe there are some things that I do not have answers to, but concerning the promises He gave in the scripture that are for me, and not yet in full manifestation in my life or ministry, I go back to Him, sit at His feet and ask Him questions, but I do not question Him.

One time, a friend reached out to me to pray for his mum. My team and I did, but she passed on still. I felt the pain in my heart, but I had two choices: conclude that God does not heal anymore or turn to God and say, "Lord, I don't know why she died but I believe what you said that we would lay hands on the sick and they will get healed, that we will raise the dead and cast out demons. Lord I believe this, and I believe I will see this happen in my lifetime. You have done some other mighty things through me and through the ministry, this won't be an exception. I will keep seeking you, praying about this, taking risks and trusting you." I chose the second option.

Over ten years ago, we got a call that one of my relatives was in a coma. They said he had a slim chance of survival. I was so strong in faith, I prayed, rejoiced and was so certain that he would live. My words and actions were in line with my faith. Other relatives at some point were concerned about me because I kept saying, "Don't worry, he won't die." Weeks later, we heard he died, but I was not moved because I remembered the case of Lazarus. A week later, my mum explained to me that I might have to let it go. I was pained and a bit confused and I prayed that the Lord would help me through it.

My point is, I have prayed for healing for a relative in a coma who died eventually, but I have also prayed and seen my father revived miraculously. I have been saved from death and calamity as well. I have seen things I cannot explain happen. We have recorded several amazing healing testimonies in the ministry. I have learnt and I am still learning to rest in His trust and never let anything drive me away from Him. Who else do I want to run to? I am too convinced of His goodness to doubt His faithfulness. Things happen but it does not make God less of Himself. I love the way Bill Johnson addresses this issue of what to do when miracles do not happen. In his book *When Heaven Invades Earth*. He said, and I paraphrase, that "do not create theologies out of your situations when miracles do not happen and do not be ashamed about it, only press-on in prayer".

What point am I trying to make? I am trying to say that you should not throw in the towel. Do not walk out on God because of disappointments, heartbreaks, unanswered prayers, or losses. Yes, the pain is real, and I am not even suggesting that we deny it, but God's love, peace, comfort and redemption is more real. He can be trusted. No one can fix a product like the producer. Nobody or nothing can satisfy or comfort us like our maker who is also our Father—God. No matter what has happened, take a risk again, accept the invitation of prayer, which means fellowship and tell Him how you feel. If there is anyone that we need to be vulnerable to, it is God. Do not let the shame, guilt or bruised ego of praying for the sick but seeing nothing happen, rob you of the potential you have been graced with. For what it is worth, if in doubt, learn and restudy how Jesus did it all.

He believed so much in you and me, little wonder he made such a bold and empowering statement in John 14:12, “Most assuredly, I say to you, he who believes in Me, the works that I do he will do also; and greater works than these he will do, because I go to My Father.”

Thank God it was Jesus Christ who said it, because if He said it, then we have been empowered to do it. We must not let the devil manipulate or condemn us because of the failures we see; rather, they should push us closer to God until we become like Him and do the greater works, no matter what it takes.

Accept the invitation to fellowship and pray today and ensure you have fun while at it because Jesus is fun to be with.

Always remember: Prayer looks good on you.

[illegible] John 14:12 [illegible] believes in Me [illegible] greater works than these [illegible] go to My Father.

[illegible]

ADDITIONAL CHAPTER RESOURCES

Extracts from The School of Intercession "Module 1" Manual

1. The Name of Jesus – The Mystery in The Name (The power in the name of Jesus and the access it offers).

Understanding the power in the name is the beginning and end of warfare. It is a victorious name. He served to attain the power in that name even though He is God. He earned it and bestowed it upon us. What a great privilege. Philippians 2:5–11 gives us a clearer perspective. When we call on the name of Jesus in prayers, we engage the highest name that triggers results. Every knee in heaven, on earth, and under the earth must bow down and every tongue must confess. What a name. We short change ourselves if we are not expectant when we call on that name.

The Scriptures also say that the name of the Lord is a strong tower, the righteous runs into it and is saved (Proverbs 18:10). Peter and John also engaged the name of the lord at beautiful gate (Acts 3:6). The question is: are you engaging the name of Jesus? Are you expectant when you call that name? Do you have a revelation of what happens when the Name is called? A little more you can do to get your name exalted is to serve, that is, do what God tells you to do. I love how Hebrews 12:2–4 describes what Jesus Christ went through to attain that powerful name. He went through it all. Do not give up on your process of becoming.

2. The Blood of Jesus

Without the blood of Jesus, we would not be having this conversation. The blood of Jesus was made available upon the death of Jesus. What a huge sacrifice just to reconcile us back to the Father. The blood does not just wash all our sins, it is a weapon of victory for any warfare (Hebrews 9:22).

Let's take a journey back to the days of the law when this mystery was enacted, that is, the law of first mention (Exodus 12:1–13). Inserted below is an excerpt from Joyce Meyer's Study Bible on the application of the blood.

God instructed the Israelites to use the blood of a lamb as a token or sign that they were not to be harmed under the Old Covenant. Notice that the Lord said to them, "When I see the blood, I will pass over you," (Exodus 12:13). In order for the people to be protected from the angel of death, God had to see the blood, and He could not see it if they did not put it on the side posts and tops of their doorframes.

You and I live under the New Covenant, which is far better than the Old Covenant because the applied blood of Jesus is permanent (see Hebrews 9:12–26). How do we "put" the blood on our lives and homes? We do it by believing in Jesus Christ as we simply say in faith, "I believe that the blood of Jesus is on my life and my home, cleansing and protecting me." We can apply the blood in any practical situation we face.

Start applying the blood by faith over yourself and that which belongs to you – your children, your car, your home, your body. Are you battling with wounded emotions? Cover your emotions with the blood of Jesus so that you will stop being devastated by people who do not seem to know how to give you what you feel you need from them. Are you in financial difficulty?

Lay your hands on your tithe cheques, your cheque books and wallets; pray that they will be protected by the blood of Jesus. Ask God to cause your money to multiply in the work of the Lord and to see to it that Satan does not steal any of it from you. Are you sick? Release your faith for the blood of Jesus to cover and protect your body. The life is in the blood; it cleanses us from all sins and protects us from the things that will harm us.

Pray with me: "Father, I come to you in Jesus' name and I apply the blood of Jesus to my life, to all that belongs to me and to everything you have given me to steward. I put the blood of Jesus on my mind, my emotions and my will. I put the blood on my family, my co-workers and my friends. Thank you for protecting me with your blood. Amen."

Also, see Hebrews 11:28, 1 Corinthians 5:7. The blood protects, covers, heals, forgives, and redeems. It is multidimensional. How pleasant it will be if we can fully understand what the blood offers and how to engage it in prayers.

Engaging the Blood of Jesus

- You must believe in the efficacy of the blood. We are victorious through the blood. Seek revelation (James 1:5, Rev 12:11).
- Through the communion, we engage the mystery of the blood of Jesus by partaking in the flesh and blood of Jesus as illustrated in the Scriptures (Matthew 26:26–28, 1 Corinthians 11:24–26). I love the phrase, "This do, as often as you drink it, in remembrance of me." We engage the covenant of the flesh and blood in remembrance of our redemption, restoration, healing, victory and all our benefits in Christ Jesus.
- You can plead the blood of Jesus over your life, situation, and so on with an understanding of the power of the blood.
- Search the Scriptures with the help of the Holy Spirit to reveal more about the power in the blood of Jesus.

3. The Word

I love the Word of God. We cannot explain or understand the Word without using the Word to explain it. It is better caught as a revelation than taught. I pray you catch the revelation of the power in the Word and how it is an infallible weapon of warfare and daily living.

I love the way Hebrews 4:12 explains the word. The Word of God is "active, full of power, operative, energising, effective, and sharper than two-edged sword" (Amplified version). What a definition.

Here are other descriptions of the Word:

- The world was framed by the word of God (Hebrews 11:3).
- In the beginning was the word (John 1:1–5).
- The words that I speak are spirit and life (John 6:63).
- Man shall not live by bread alone but by the word of God (Matthew 4:4).
- The word is a lamp to my feet and light to my path (Psalm 119:105).
- Do not let this book of the law depart from your mouth (Joshua 1:8).
- Whatever you bind on earth (Matthew 18:18).
- You shall decree a thing on earth, and it shall be established (Job 22:28).
- Ephesians 6:17, shows that the word of God is a part of the armour of God through which we wage war against the kingdom of darkness.

Just as God put his Words in the mouth of Jeremiah, we have the Word of God available to us, let us engage it (Jeremiah 1:9–10).

We engage the word by:

- Meditating constantly on the word (Joshua 1:8).
- Boldly declaring the word by faith (Romans 10:10).
- Hiding the word in our heart and constant renewal of our mind through the word (Psalm 119:11, Romans 12:1–2).
- Faith (James 1:6–8).

- Praying the word (Isaiah 43:26).
- Letting his word abide in you (John 15:7).

4. Partnering with the Holy Spirit and Praying in the Holy Ghost

I love Him. He is the surest standby anyone can have or ask for. We first encountered Him in Genesis 1:2 as a creative spirit. Never threatened by darkness, but can brood over it till creation occurs. In the book of John, Jesus said, "It is expedient I go, so that He can come and be with you." If Jesus says it is expedient to have the Holy Spirit then, it is *expedient* indeed (John 14:26).

He is the comforter, counsellor, helper, intercessor, advocate, strengthener, standby, and teacher that causes us to remember all things. Glory to God! See who we have in us, upon us and with us as we engage in prayers and life. Little wonder the Scriptures say that "we are more than conquerors" (Romans 8:37). The Holy Spirit helps us understand who we are thus positioning us to pray as well as praying for us. Do not forget, He is also our *intercessor* (Romans 8:14–16; 26–27).

Praying in The Holy Ghost

- Let's go back to where it started – praying in tongues – Acts 2. Note that they were waiting upon the empowerment of the Holy Ghost, and one of the outcomes was praying in the Holy Ghost. It is evidence of being filled by the Holy Ghost. Ephesians 6:18 clearly states that we should pray in the spirit. It was not invented by men but by the Holy Spirit Himself.

- Jude 1:20 tells us that you build up your faith by praying in the Holy Ghost.
- 1 Corinthians 14:4 tells us that you edify yourself.
- Romans 8:26–27 tells us that it helps you with intercession.

5. The Armour of God

No doubt, we will fight battles. We will find ourselves in wars that we will wonder how we got involved, but we must not fret because we are victorious. We know how it will end (1 John 5:4). However, like every army, we have our weapon and armour that we must wear if we want to experience the victorious life available to us.

Ephesians 6:10–18 explains it perfectly well.

> 10 Finally, my brethren, be strong in the Lord and in the power of His might.
> 11 Put on the whole armour of God, that you may be able to stand against the wiles of the devil.
> 12 For we do not wrestle against flesh and blood, but against principalities, against powers, against the rulers of the darkness of this age, against spiritual hosts of wickedness in the heavenly places.
> 13 Therefore take up the whole armour of God, that you may be able to withstand in the evil day, and having done all, to stand.
> 14 Stand therefore, having girded your waist with truth, having put on the breastplate of righteousness,

15 and having shod your feet with the preparation of the gospel of peace;
16 above all, taking the shield of faith with which, you will be able to quench all the fiery darts of the wicked one.
17 And take the helmet of salvation, and the sword of the Spirit, which is the word of God;
18 Praying always with all prayer and supplication in the Spirit, being watchful to this end with all perseverance and supplication for all the saints.

Engaging the Armour

- First, we must understand who we are up against and his nature (Ephesians 6:12). They do not respond to anything else except what God Himself prescribed. We cannot approach these battles with just our intellect.
- We are to put on this armour at all times. We don't pick the ones we like and toss away the ones we don't like or understand.
- Understand that the armour delivers victory.

RECOMMENDED BOOKS

1. The Bible: This is a must read.
2. *The Proof* by Taiwo Odukoya: This is a compilation of some testimonies. It will help build your faith in prayers. Remember stewarding your joy and testimonies as weapons for effective prayer? This book will help you with that.
3. *Hosting the Presence* by Bill Johnson:This book will help you understand how to have an effective relationship with the Holy Spirit. Remember, He is our helper, even in praying effectively.
4. *Fire brand Prayer Journal, Fire brand Book and Fire brand Psalms* by Debola Deji-Kurunmi: The journal is a good prayer resource to have. It gives you an opportunity to create a workable schedule, and have certain prayers based on the word to birth revival encounters and hunger pangs for God.
5. *Prayer: Your Foundation for Success* by Kenneth Copeland
6. *The Ministry of Intercession* by Andrew Murray.
7. Any of Andrew Wommack's books on prayer.

References

- Hope 365 School of Intercession Manual
- Joyce Meyer, *The Everyday Life Bible: The Power of God's Word for Everyday Living* (New York, FaithWords, 2013)

ACKNOWLEDGEMENT

I would like to express my heartfelt gratitude to Olumide Owolabi, my husband and best friend, for letting me soar and pushing me to be the kind of woman I am destined to be. He has continually served as my voice of reason and daily reminder that God loves me. Thank you for picking up their call (he knows what I mean).

To my spiritual father, Pastor Taiwo Odukoya, thank you for showing and teaching me what it means to live a life devoted to God.

Tola Omoniyi, thank you for sending me that picture of yourself that was supposed to make me tease you; rather, it inspired the idea for this book.

Oluwatoni Abraham and Mojisola Ogunlola, thank you angels for your help in polishing the ideas in this book. Kemi Odukoya, thank you for helping me make sense of my ideas in its earlier rough draft. It could only have been you.

Tolulope Falola, thank you for your unwavering prayers and support and for holding my hands throughout the process of this book.

To my amazing personal assistant, Maureen Odidison, thank you for walking with me on this journey.

Adenike Oyetunde, you are an angel. Thank you for

insisting I buy a particular book which led me to Anwuli's office.

Anwuli Ojogwu, I bless the day I walked into your office. Aside from your excellent work ethic, thank you for believing in this project, consistently speaking words of encouragement and taking this work like it's yours. Thank you.

To my family, loved ones, colleagues and everyone who kept fanning the flames of prayer within me, I appreciate you.

ABOUT THE AUTHOR

IMISIOLUWA OWOLABI is the President of "Hope365" and the "WhenFriendsPray" platform. She is an international speaker, author and life coach. Through her work, she has transformed lives and businesses. She is also the Lead Trainer/Strategist at "DreamsMeetStrategy" and the host of a weekly radio programme, "Everything Love", which has earned international recognition and won an award in 2017 from Domestic Violence, UK for its contributions to emotional stability.

She is the writer and narrator of the audiobook, *Psalms by Imisi*, which is a compilation of thoughts, poems, prayers, expressions and conversations with God. In 2004, she became a trainer through her role as a peer educator with Family Health International (FHI). Imisi is also a certified coach and strategist with over ten years of experience, and she has birthed and coordinated over ninety life-transforming events and projects within the last decade.

She is married to her best friend, Olumide Owolabi. Above all, her highest status remains "Child of God".

To contact her or get more information about her projects or upcoming events, please visit: www.imisiowolabi.com.